40 Wine Recipes for Home

By: Kelly Johnson

Table of Contents

Wine Cocktails:

- Wine Spritzer
- Red Wine Manhattan
- White Wine Sangria
- Rosé Berry Fizz
- Wine Mojito
- Cherry Blossom Wine Cooler
- Blackberry Basil Smash
- Cucumber Mint Wine Refresher
- Ginger Pear Wine Fizz
- Tropical Wine Punch

Sangria Recipes:

- Classic Red Sangria
- White Peach Sangria
- Sparkling Rosé Sangria
- Citrus Mint Sangria
- Autumn Apple Sangria
- Summer Berry Sangria
- Watermelon Mint Sangria
- Citrus Rosé Sangria
- Cranberry Apple Sangria
- Minty Peach Sangria

Wine Slushies:

- Strawberry Wine Slush
- Peach Bellini Wine Slush
- Mango Moscato Slush
- Blueberry Lemon Wine Slush
- Raspberry Rosé Slushie
- Mango Strawberry Wine Slush

Unique Wine Beverages:

- Mulled Wine
- Wine Ice Pops
- Wine Smoothie
- Savory Wine Spritz
- Wine Hot Chocolate
- Wine Slush Float
- Spicy Jalapeño Wine Margarita
- Lemon Lavender Wine Spritz
- Wine Infused Lemonade
- Balsamic Berry Wine Reduction
- Wine-soaked Berries with Mascarpone
- Hibiscus Rosé Punch
- Pomegranate Wine Spritzer
- Chocolate Red Wine Truffles

Wine Cocktails:
Wine Spritzer

Ingredients:

- 4 ounces of white or red wine (choose a wine you enjoy)
- 4 ounces of club soda or sparkling water
- Ice cubes
- Optional: a wedge of lemon or lime for garnish

Instructions:

Fill a glass with ice cubes.
Pour 4 ounces of your chosen wine into the glass.
Top it off with 4 ounces of club soda or sparkling water. Adjust the ratio according to your preference, adding more or less soda to achieve your desired strength.
Gently stir the mixture to combine the wine and soda.
Optionally, garnish with a wedge of lemon or lime for a citrusy twist.
Enjoy your refreshing wine spritzer!

You can customize your wine spritzer by experimenting with different types of wine, such as a crisp white wine or a fruity red. Additionally, you can add fresh fruit slices, berries, or herbs like mint to enhance the flavor. Adjust the ratios to suit your taste and create your own signature spritzer.

Red Wine Manhattan

Ingredients:

- 2 ounces bourbon or rye whiskey
- 1 ounce red wine (choose a robust red wine like a Cabernet Sauvignon or Merlot)
- 1/2 ounce sweet vermouth
- 1 dash Angostura bitters
- Orange peel or cherry for garnish

Instructions:

Fill a mixing glass with ice.
Add the bourbon or rye whiskey, red wine, sweet vermouth, and a dash of Angostura bitters to the mixing glass.
Stir the ingredients well to chill the mixture. Stirring is preferred over shaking to maintain the clarity of the drink.
Strain the mixture into a chilled cocktail glass.
Express the oil from an orange peel over the drink by holding it over the glass and giving it a twist, then drop the peel into the glass. Alternatively, you can garnish with a cherry.
Enjoy your Red Wine Manhattan!

This cocktail combines the richness of red wine with the warmth of bourbon or rye, resulting in a complex and flavorful drink. Feel free to adjust the ratios to suit your taste preferences, and experiment with different types of red wine to find the combination you like best.

White Wine Sangria

Ingredients:

- 1 bottle (750 ml) of white wine (such as Sauvignon Blanc or Pinot Grigio)
- 1/4 cup brandy
- 2 tablespoons sugar (adjust to taste)
- 1 orange, sliced
- 1 lemon, sliced
- 1 lime, sliced
- 1 peach or nectarine, sliced
- 1/2 cup strawberries, hulled and halved
- 1-2 cups sparkling water or club soda (adjust to your preferred level of fizziness)
- Ice cubes

Optional Garnishes:

- Fresh mint leaves
- Additional fruit slices for garnish

Instructions:

In a large pitcher, combine the white wine and brandy.
Add the sugar to the pitcher and stir until it dissolves. Adjust the sweetness to your liking.
Add the sliced orange, lemon, lime, peach or nectarine, and strawberries to the pitcher. You can also add other fruits like grapes or berries, depending on your preference.
Place the pitcher in the refrigerator and let the mixture chill for at least 2-4 hours, allowing the flavors to meld.
Just before serving, add the sparkling water or club soda to the pitcher. Adjust the amount to achieve your desired level of effervescence.
Stir the sangria gently to mix everything together.
Serve the White Wine Sangria over ice in individual glasses, making sure to include some fruit in each serving.
Optionally, garnish each glass with fresh mint leaves or additional fruit slices.

Enjoy your refreshing White Wine Sangria! Feel free to customize the recipe by adding your favorite fruits or experimenting with different types of white wine.

Rosé Berry Fizz

Ingredients:

- 4 ounces rosé wine (chilled)
- 1 ounce berry liqueur (such as Chambord or cassis)
- 1/2 ounce simple syrup (adjust to taste)
- 1/2 ounce freshly squeezed lemon juice
- Club soda or sparkling water
- Fresh berries (strawberries, raspberries, blueberries) for garnish
- Ice cubes

Instructions:

Fill a glass with ice cubes.
In a cocktail shaker, combine the rosé wine, berry liqueur, simple syrup, and freshly squeezed lemon juice.
Shake the mixture well to chill the ingredients.
Strain the mixture into the prepared glass over ice.
Top off the glass with club soda or sparkling water to add effervescence. Adjust the amount to your preference.
Gently stir the cocktail to combine the ingredients.
Garnish the drink with fresh berries.
Enjoy your Rosé Berry Fizz!

Feel free to experiment with the berry liqueur and adjust the sweetness to suit your taste. This cocktail is not only visually appealing with its vibrant colors but also offers a delightful blend of flavors. Cheers!

Wine Mojito

Ingredients:

- 1 cup white wine (such as Sauvignon Blanc or Pinot Grigio), chilled
- 1 tablespoon sugar (adjust to taste)
- 1/2 lime, cut into wedges
- Fresh mint leaves
- Soda water or club soda
- Ice cubes

Instructions:

In a glass, muddle together the sugar, lime wedges, and a handful of fresh mint leaves. Muddling involves gently pressing the ingredients to release their flavors.
Fill the glass with ice cubes.
Pour the chilled white wine over the ice.
Top off the glass with soda water or club soda, adjusting the amount to your desired level of fizziness.
Stir the mixture gently to combine the ingredients.
Garnish the drink with additional lime wedges and mint leaves.
Optionally, you can add a splash of simple syrup if you prefer a sweeter taste.
Enjoy your refreshing Wine Mojito!

This cocktail offers a crisp and fruity take on the classic Mojito, making it a perfect choice for those who enjoy wine-based drinks. Feel free to adjust the ingredients and proportions based on your personal taste preferences. Cheers!

Cherry Blossom Wine Cooler

Ingredients:

- 4 ounces rosé wine (chilled)
- 1 ounce cherry liqueur (such as cherry brandy or cherry liqueur)
- 1/2 ounce elderflower liqueur
- 1/2 ounce freshly squeezed lemon juice
- Club soda or sparkling water
- Fresh cherries for garnish
- Ice cubes

Instructions:

Fill a wine glass with ice cubes.
In a mixing glass, combine the chilled rosé wine, cherry liqueur, elderflower liqueur, and freshly squeezed lemon juice.
Stir the mixture well to combine the ingredients.
Strain the mixture into the prepared wine glass over ice.
Top off the glass with club soda or sparkling water, adjusting the amount to your preference.
Gently stir the cocktail to incorporate the bubbly water.
Garnish the drink with fresh cherries.
Enjoy your Cherry Blossom Wine Cooler!

This cocktail offers a perfect balance of floral and fruity notes with the refreshing touch of sparkling water. It's a lovely and elegant drink, perfect for warm weather or any festive occasion. Adjust the ingredients based on your taste preferences and enjoy the delightful flavors of the Cherry Blossom Wine Cooler. Cheers!

Blackberry Basil Smash

Ingredients:

- 2 ounces gin
- 1/2 cup fresh blackberries
- 1/2 ounce simple syrup (adjust to taste)
- 1 ounce freshly squeezed lemon juice
- Fresh basil leaves
- Ice cubes

Instructions:

In a cocktail shaker, muddle the fresh blackberries and a few basil leaves.
Add the gin, simple syrup, and freshly squeezed lemon juice to the shaker.
Fill the shaker with ice cubes.
Shake the mixture vigorously for about 15-20 seconds to chill the ingredients.
Strain the mixture into a glass filled with ice.
Garnish with additional blackberries and fresh basil leaves.
Optionally, you can double-strain the mixture to remove pulp and seeds if you prefer a smoother texture.
Enjoy your Blackberry Basil Smash!

This cocktail offers a delightful combination of fruity sweetness, herbal freshness, and a hint of tartness from the lemon juice. Adjust the simple syrup to achieve your desired level of sweetness. It's a perfect choice for warm days or as a refreshing evening cocktail. Cheers!

Cucumber Mint Wine Refresher

Ingredients:

- 1 cup white wine (such as Sauvignon Blanc or Pinot Grigio), chilled
- 1/4 cup cucumber, thinly sliced
- Fresh mint leaves
- 1 tablespoon simple syrup (adjust to taste)
- 1/2 lime, juiced
- Club soda or sparkling water
- Ice cubes

Instructions:

In a mixing glass or pitcher, combine the chilled white wine, cucumber slices, fresh mint leaves, simple syrup, and lime juice.
Stir the mixture gently to combine the ingredients.
Fill a glass with ice cubes.
Pour the wine mixture over the ice in the glass.
Top off the glass with club soda or sparkling water, adjusting the amount to your liking.
Stir the drink gently to incorporate the bubbly water.
Garnish with additional cucumber slices and mint leaves.
Enjoy your Cucumber Mint Wine Refresher!

This cocktail offers a wonderful combination of the bright flavors of cucumber and mint, complemented by the crispness of white wine. Feel free to adjust the simple syrup and lime juice to achieve your preferred level of sweetness and tartness. It's a perfect choice for a light and revitalizing beverage. Cheers!

Ginger Pear Wine Fizz

Ingredients:

- 1 cup white wine (such as Pinot Grigio or Chardonnay), chilled
- 1/4 cup pear nectar or pear juice
- 1 tablespoon fresh ginger, grated or muddled
- 1 tablespoon honey or simple syrup (adjust to taste)
- 1/2 lime, juiced
- Club soda or ginger beer
- Ice cubes
- Slices of fresh pear for garnish

Instructions:

In a mixing glass or pitcher, combine the chilled white wine, pear nectar or juice, grated or muddled ginger, honey or simple syrup, and lime juice.
Stir the mixture well to infuse the flavors.
Fill a glass with ice cubes.
Pour the wine mixture over the ice in the glass.
Top off the glass with club soda or ginger beer, adjusting the amount to your liking.
Stir the drink gently to combine the ingredients.
Garnish with slices of fresh pear.
Enjoy your Ginger Pear Wine Fizz!

This cocktail offers a harmonious blend of pear sweetness with the spicy kick of ginger, all enhanced by the effervescence of the white wine and soda. Adjust the sweetness and ginger intensity to suit your taste preferences. It's a refreshing and flavorful option for a variety of occasions. Cheers!

Tropical Wine Punch

Ingredients:

- 1 bottle (750 ml) white wine (such as Sauvignon Blanc or Pinot Grigio), chilled
- 1 cup pineapple juice
- 1/2 cup orange juice
- 1/4 cup coconut rum
- 2 tablespoons simple syrup (adjust to taste)
- Assorted tropical fruits (pineapple chunks, mango slices, kiwi slices, orange slices, etc.)
- Club soda or sparkling water
- Ice cubes
- Fresh mint leaves for garnish

Instructions:

In a large pitcher, combine the chilled white wine, pineapple juice, orange juice, coconut rum, and simple syrup.
Stir the mixture well to ensure all ingredients are thoroughly mixed.
Add the assorted tropical fruits to the pitcher. You can use a combination of pineapple chunks, mango slices, kiwi slices, and orange slices. Stir to distribute the fruits evenly.
Place the pitcher in the refrigerator and let it chill for at least 2-4 hours, allowing the flavors to meld.
Just before serving, add club soda or sparkling water to the pitcher to add a refreshing fizziness. Adjust the amount to your preference.
Fill glasses with ice cubes.
Pour the Tropical Wine Punch into the glasses, making sure to include some of the fruit pieces.
Garnish each glass with fresh mint leaves.
Stir gently and enjoy your Tropical Wine Punch!

This punch is not only visually appealing with its colorful fruits but also offers a taste of the tropics in every sip. Feel free to customize the recipe with your favorite tropical fruits and adjust the sweetness to your liking. It's perfect for summer gatherings and parties. Cheers!

Sangria Recipes:

Classic Red Sangria:

Ingredients:

- 1 bottle (750 ml) red wine (such as Tempranillo or Garnacha)
- 1/4 cup brandy
- 1/4 cup orange liqueur (e.g., triple sec)
- 2 tablespoons sugar (adjust to taste)
- 1 orange, sliced
- 1 lemon, sliced
- 2 tablespoons freshly squeezed orange juice
- 1-2 cups soda water or club soda
- Ice cubes
- Additional fruits for garnish (berries, cherries, etc.)

Instructions:

In a large pitcher, combine the red wine, brandy, orange liqueur, and sugar. Stir until the sugar dissolves.
Add the sliced orange, sliced lemon, and freshly squeezed orange juice to the pitcher. Stir to combine.
Place the pitcher in the refrigerator and let the mixture chill for at least 2-4 hours to allow the flavors to meld.
Just before serving, add soda water or club soda to the pitcher for a fizzy touch. Adjust the amount to your preference.
Fill glasses with ice cubes and pour the Sangria over the ice.
Garnish with additional fruits.
Stir gently and serve your Classic Red Sangria.

White Sangria:

Ingredients:

- 1 bottle (750 ml) white wine (such as Albariño or Sauvignon Blanc)
- 1/4 cup peach schnapps
- 2 tablespoons sugar (adjust to taste)
- 1 peach, sliced
- 1 green apple, sliced
- 1 lemon, sliced
- 2 tablespoons freshly squeezed lemon juice
- 1-2 cups ginger ale or lemon-lime soda
- Ice cubes
- Fresh mint leaves for garnish

Instructions:

In a large pitcher, combine the white wine, peach schnapps, and sugar. Stir until the sugar dissolves.

Add the sliced peach, sliced green apple, sliced lemon, and freshly squeezed lemon juice to the pitcher. Stir to combine.

Place the pitcher in the refrigerator and let the mixture chill for at least 2-4 hours to allow the flavors to meld.

Just before serving, add ginger ale or lemon-lime soda to the pitcher for a bubbly element. Adjust the amount to your preference.

Fill glasses with ice cubes and pour the White Sangria over the ice.

Garnish with fresh mint leaves.

Stir gently and serve your White Sangria.

Feel free to customize these recipes by adding your favorite fruits and adjusting the sweetness levels to suit your taste. Enjoy your Sangria!

Classic Red Sangria

Ingredients:

- 1 bottle (750 ml) red wine (such as Tempranillo or Garnacha)
- 1/4 cup brandy
- 1/4 cup orange liqueur (e.g., triple sec)
- 2 tablespoons sugar (adjust to taste)
- 1 orange, sliced
- 1 lemon, sliced
- 1 lime, sliced
- 2 tablespoons freshly squeezed orange juice
- 2 tablespoons freshly squeezed lemon juice
- 2 tablespoons freshly squeezed lime juice
- 1-2 cups soda water or club soda
- Ice cubes
- Additional fruits for garnish (berries, cherries, etc.)

Instructions:

In a large pitcher, combine the red wine, brandy, orange liqueur, and sugar. Stir until the sugar dissolves.
Add the sliced orange, sliced lemon, sliced lime, freshly squeezed orange juice, freshly squeezed lemon juice, and freshly squeezed lime juice to the pitcher. Stir to combine.
Place the pitcher in the refrigerator and let the mixture chill for at least 2-4 hours to allow the flavors to meld.
Just before serving, add soda water or club soda to the pitcher for a fizzy touch. Adjust the amount to your preference.
Fill glasses with ice cubes and pour the Sangria over the ice.
Garnish with additional fruits.
Stir gently and serve your Classic Red Sangria.

Feel free to customize the recipe by adding your favorite fruits or adjusting the sweetness to your liking. Classic red sangria is perfect for gatherings and parties, and it's best enjoyed chilled on a warm day. Cheers!

White Peach Sangria

Ingredients:

- 1 bottle (750 ml) white wine (such as Pinot Grigio or Sauvignon Blanc), chilled
- 1/4 cup peach schnapps
- 2 tablespoons sugar (adjust to taste)
- 3 ripe white peaches, sliced
- 1 lemon, sliced
- 1 lime, sliced
- 1-2 cups ginger ale or lemon-lime soda
- Ice cubes
- Fresh mint leaves for garnish

Instructions:

In a large pitcher, combine the chilled white wine, peach schnapps, and sugar. Stir until the sugar dissolves.

Add the sliced white peaches, sliced lemon, and sliced lime to the pitcher. Stir gently to combine.

Place the pitcher in the refrigerator and let the mixture chill for at least 2-4 hours to allow the flavors to meld.

Just before serving, add ginger ale or lemon-lime soda to the pitcher for a bubbly element. Adjust the amount to your preference.

Fill glasses with ice cubes and pour the White Peach Sangria over the ice.

Garnish with fresh mint leaves.

Stir gently and serve your White Peach Sangria.

Feel free to customize the recipe by adding other fruits like berries or grapes, and adjust the sweetness level according to your taste. White Peach Sangria is a perfect choice for summer gatherings, brunches, or any festive occasion. Enjoy!

Sparkling Rosé Sangria

Ingredients:

- 1 bottle (750 ml) sparkling rosé wine, chilled
- 1/4 cup elderflower liqueur
- 2 tablespoons sugar (adjust to taste)
- 1 cup mixed berries (strawberries, raspberries, blueberries)
- 1 orange, thinly sliced
- 1 lemon, thinly sliced
- 1 peach or nectarine, sliced
- 1-2 cups sparkling water or club soda
- Ice cubes
- Fresh mint leaves for garnish

Instructions:

In a large pitcher, combine the chilled sparkling rosé wine, elderflower liqueur, and sugar. Stir until the sugar dissolves.

Add the mixed berries, orange slices, lemon slices, and peach or nectarine slices to the pitcher. Stir gently to combine.

Place the pitcher in the refrigerator and let the mixture chill for at least 2-4 hours to allow the flavors to meld.

Just before serving, add sparkling water or club soda to the pitcher for extra effervescence. Adjust the amount to your preference.

Fill glasses with ice cubes and pour the Sparkling Rosé Sangria over the ice. Garnish with fresh mint leaves.

Stir gently and serve your Sparkling Rosé Sangria.

Feel free to customize the recipe by adding other fruits or herbs based on your preference. Sparkling Rosé Sangria is perfect for brunches, celebrations, or any occasion where you want to enjoy a light and bubbly beverage. Cheers!

Citrus Mint Sangria

Ingredients:

- 1 bottle (750 ml) white wine (such as Sauvignon Blanc or Pinot Grigio), chilled
- 1/4 cup orange liqueur (e.g., triple sec)
- 2 tablespoons honey or simple syrup (adjust to taste)
- 1 orange, thinly sliced
- 1 lemon, thinly sliced
- 1 lime, thinly sliced
- 1 grapefruit, thinly sliced
- 1/2 cup fresh mint leaves
- 1-2 cups sparkling water or club soda
- Ice cubes
- Additional citrus slices and mint sprigs for garnish

Instructions:

In a large pitcher, combine the chilled white wine, orange liqueur, and honey or simple syrup. Stir until the sweetener dissolves.
Add the sliced orange, sliced lemon, sliced lime, sliced grapefruit, and fresh mint leaves to the pitcher. Stir gently to combine.
Place the pitcher in the refrigerator and let the mixture chill for at least 2-4 hours to allow the flavors to meld.
Just before serving, add sparkling water or club soda to the pitcher for a fizzy touch. Adjust the amount to your preference.
Fill glasses with ice cubes and pour the Citrus Mint Sangria over the ice.
Garnish with additional citrus slices and mint sprigs.
Stir gently and serve your Citrus Mint Sangria.

Feel free to customize the recipe by adding other citrus fruits or berries if desired. This sangria is perfect for warm days, picnics, or any occasion where you want to enjoy a citrusy and refreshing beverage. Cheers!

Autumn Apple Sangria

Ingredients:

- 1 bottle (750 ml) red wine (such as Tempranillo or Merlot), chilled
- 1 cup apple cider
- 1/4 cup brandy
- 2 tablespoons maple syrup or honey (adjust to taste)
- 2 apples, cored and thinly sliced (use a mix of red and green apples)
- 1 pear, cored and thinly sliced
- 1 cinnamon stick
- 1/2 teaspoon ground cinnamon
- 1/4 teaspoon ground nutmeg
- 1-2 cups sparkling water or ginger ale
- Ice cubes
- Additional apple slices and cinnamon sticks for garnish

Instructions:

In a large pitcher, combine the chilled red wine, apple cider, brandy, and maple syrup or honey. Stir until the sweetener dissolves.
Add the sliced apples, sliced pear, cinnamon stick, ground cinnamon, and ground nutmeg to the pitcher. Stir gently to combine.
Place the pitcher in the refrigerator and let the mixture chill for at least 2-4 hours to allow the flavors to meld.
Just before serving, add sparkling water or ginger ale to the pitcher for a fizzy touch. Adjust the amount to your preference.
Fill glasses with ice cubes and pour the Autumn Apple Sangria over the ice.
Garnish with additional apple slices and cinnamon sticks.
Stir gently and serve your Autumn Apple Sangria.

Feel free to customize the recipe by adding a splash of orange juice or including other fall fruits like cranberries. This sangria is perfect for autumn gatherings, Thanksgiving celebrations, or any occasion where you want to savor the flavors of the season. Cheers!

Summer Berry Sangria

Ingredients:

- 1 bottle (750 ml) red wine (such as a fruity Merlot or Zinfandel), chilled
- 1/4 cup brandy
- 2 tablespoons sugar (adjust to taste)
- 1 cup strawberries, hulled and halved
- 1 cup blueberries
- 1 cup raspberries
- 1 cup blackberries
- 1 orange, thinly sliced
- 1 lemon, thinly sliced
- 1-2 cups berry-flavored soda or club soda
- Ice cubes
- Fresh mint leaves for garnish

Instructions:

In a large pitcher, combine the chilled red wine, brandy, and sugar. Stir until the sugar dissolves.
Add the strawberries, blueberries, raspberries, blackberries, sliced orange, and sliced lemon to the pitcher. Stir gently to combine.
Place the pitcher in the refrigerator and let the mixture chill for at least 2-4 hours to allow the flavors to meld.
Just before serving, add berry-flavored soda or club soda to the pitcher for a fizzy touch. Adjust the amount to your preference.
Fill glasses with ice cubes and pour the Summer Berry Sangria over the ice.
Garnish with fresh mint leaves.
Stir gently and serve your Summer Berry Sangria.

Feel free to customize the recipe by adding other summer fruits like peaches, nectarines, or kiwi. This sangria is perfect for warm days, picnics, or any summer celebration where you want to enjoy the vibrant flavors of seasonal berries. Cheers!

Watermelon Mint Sangria

Ingredients:

- 1 small seedless watermelon, diced (about 4 cups)
- 1 bottle (750 ml) white wine (such as Sauvignon Blanc or Pinot Grigio), chilled
- 1/4 cup vodka
- 1/4 cup triple sec or orange liqueur
- 2-3 tablespoons honey or simple syrup (adjust to taste)
- 1 lime, thinly sliced
- Fresh mint leaves (about 1/2 cup)
- 1-2 cups sparkling water or club soda
- Ice cubes
- Additional watermelon cubes and mint sprigs for garnish

Instructions:

In a blender, puree the diced watermelon until smooth. Strain the puree to remove pulp, if desired.
In a large pitcher, combine the chilled white wine, vodka, triple sec, and honey or simple syrup. Stir until the sweetener dissolves.
Add the watermelon puree, lime slices, and fresh mint leaves to the pitcher. Stir gently to combine.
Place the pitcher in the refrigerator and let the mixture chill for at least 2-4 hours to allow the flavors to meld.
Just before serving, add sparkling water or club soda to the pitcher for a fizzy touch. Adjust the amount to your preference.
Fill glasses with ice cubes and pour the Watermelon Mint Sangria over the ice. Garnish with additional watermelon cubes and mint sprigs.
Stir gently and serve your Watermelon Mint Sangria.

Feel free to customize the recipe by adding a splash of lemon or lime juice, or even a hint of ginger for extra zing. This sangria is perfect for summer parties, barbecues, or any occasion where you want to enjoy a refreshing and fruity drink. Cheers!

Citrus Rosé Sangria

Ingredients:

- 1 bottle (750 ml) rosé wine, chilled
- 1/4 cup orange liqueur (e.g., triple sec)
- 2 tablespoons sugar (adjust to taste)
- 1 orange, thinly sliced
- 1 lemon, thinly sliced
- 1 lime, thinly sliced
- 1 grapefruit, thinly sliced
- 1/4 cup fresh orange juice
- 1-2 cups sparkling water or club soda
- Ice cubes
- Fresh mint leaves for garnish

Instructions:

In a large pitcher, combine the chilled rosé wine, orange liqueur, and sugar. Stir until the sugar dissolves.
Add the sliced orange, sliced lemon, sliced lime, sliced grapefruit, and fresh orange juice to the pitcher. Stir gently to combine.
Place the pitcher in the refrigerator and let the mixture chill for at least 2-4 hours to allow the flavors to meld.
Just before serving, add sparkling water or club soda to the pitcher for a fizzy touch. Adjust the amount to your preference.
Fill glasses with ice cubes and pour the Citrus Rosé Sangria over the ice.
Garnish with fresh mint leaves.
Stir gently and serve your Citrus Rosé Sangria.

Feel free to customize the recipe by adding other citrus fruits such as blood oranges or tangerines. This sangria is perfect for warm days, brunches, or any occasion where you want to enjoy the bright and citrusy flavors of summer. Cheers!

Cranberry Apple Sangria

Ingredients:

- 1 bottle (750 ml) red wine (such as Merlot or Cabernet Sauvignon), chilled
- 1 cup cranberry juice
- 1/2 cup brandy
- 1/4 cup orange liqueur (e.g., triple sec)
- 1/4 cup honey or maple syrup (adjust to taste)
- 2 apples, cored and thinly sliced (use a mix of red and green apples)
- 1 cup fresh cranberries
- 1 orange, thinly sliced
- 1 cinnamon stick
- 1-2 cups club soda or sparkling water
- Ice cubes
- Additional cranberries and apple slices for garnish

Instructions:

In a large pitcher, combine the chilled red wine, cranberry juice, brandy, orange liqueur, and honey or maple syrup. Stir until the sweetener dissolves.
Add the sliced apples, fresh cranberries, sliced orange, and cinnamon stick to the pitcher. Stir gently to combine.
Place the pitcher in the refrigerator and let the mixture chill for at least 2-4 hours to allow the flavors to meld.
Just before serving, add club soda or sparkling water to the pitcher for a fizzy touch. Adjust the amount to your preference.
Fill glasses with ice cubes and pour the Cranberry Apple Sangria over the ice.
Garnish with additional cranberries and apple slices.
Stir gently and serve your Cranberry Apple Sangria.

Feel free to customize the recipe by adding a splash of cranberry-flavored vodka or orange juice if you'd like an extra fruity kick. This sangria is perfect for holiday celebrations, Thanksgiving, or any cozy gathering during the colder months. Cheers!

Minty Peach Sangria

Ingredients:

- 1 bottle (750 ml) white wine (such as Pinot Grigio or Sauvignon Blanc), chilled
- 1/4 cup peach schnapps
- 2 tablespoons sugar (adjust to taste)
- 3 ripe peaches, sliced
- 1/2 cup fresh mint leaves
- 1 lemon, thinly sliced
- 1 lime, thinly sliced
- 1-2 cups ginger ale or sparkling water
- Ice cubes
- Additional peach slices and mint sprigs for garnish

Instructions:

In a large pitcher, combine the chilled white wine, peach schnapps, and sugar. Stir until the sugar dissolves.

Add the sliced peaches, fresh mint leaves, sliced lemon, and sliced lime to the pitcher. Stir gently to combine.

Place the pitcher in the refrigerator and let the mixture chill for at least 2-4 hours to allow the flavors to meld.

Just before serving, add ginger ale or sparkling water to the pitcher for a fizzy touch. Adjust the amount to your preference.

Fill glasses with ice cubes and pour the Minty Peach Sangria over the ice.

Garnish with additional peach slices and mint sprigs.

Stir gently and serve your Minty Peach Sangria.

Feel free to customize the recipe by adding a splash of peach-flavored vodka or a hint of lemon juice for extra brightness. This sangria is perfect for summer picnics, brunches, or any occasion where you want to enjoy a light and minty peach-infused beverage. Cheers!

Wine Slushies:

Strawberry Wine Slush

Ingredients:

- 2 cups frozen strawberries
- 1 bottle (750 ml) white wine (such as a fruity Riesling or Moscato), chilled
- 2-3 tablespoons sugar (adjust to taste)
- 1-2 tablespoons lemon juice
- Ice cubes (optional)
- Fresh strawberries for garnish

Instructions:

Place the frozen strawberries in a blender.
Pour the chilled white wine into the blender with the strawberries.
Add sugar and lemon juice to the blender.
Blend the mixture until smooth and slushy.
Taste the slush and adjust the sugar and lemon juice if needed.
If a thicker consistency is desired, add ice cubes and blend again until smooth.
Pour the Strawberry Wine Slush into glasses.
Garnish with fresh strawberries.
Serve immediately and enjoy your Strawberry Wine Slush!

Feel free to customize the recipe by using different types of white wine or adding a splash of strawberry liqueur for extra flavor. This refreshing slush is perfect for warm days or as a fun and fruity drink for gatherings. Cheers!

Peach Bellini Wine Slush

Ingredients:

- 2 cups frozen peaches
- 1 bottle (750 ml) sparkling wine or Prosecco, chilled
- 2-3 tablespoons peach schnapps
- 2 tablespoons sugar (adjust to taste)
- 1-2 tablespoons lemon juice
- Ice cubes (optional)
- Fresh peach slices for garnish

Instructions:

Place the frozen peaches in a blender.
Pour the chilled sparkling wine or Prosecco into the blender with the peaches.
Add peach schnapps, sugar, and lemon juice to the blender.
Blend the mixture until smooth and slushy.
Taste the slush and adjust the sugar and lemon juice if needed.
If a thicker consistency is desired, add ice cubes and blend again until smooth.
Pour the Peach Bellini Wine Slush into glasses.
Garnish with fresh peach slices.
Serve immediately and enjoy your Peach Bellini Wine Slush!

Feel free to customize the recipe by using different types of sparkling wine or adding a splash of peach liqueur for extra peachy goodness. This frozen treat is perfect for summer parties, brunches, or any occasion where you want to savor the flavors of peach and bubbly wine. Cheers!

Mango Moscato Slush

Ingredients:

- 2 cups frozen mango chunks
- 1 bottle (750 ml) Moscato wine, chilled
- 2 tablespoons honey or agave syrup (adjust to taste)
- 1-2 tablespoons lime juice
- Ice cubes (optional)
- Fresh mango slices for garnish

Instructions:

Place the frozen mango chunks in a blender.
Pour the chilled Moscato wine into the blender with the mango.
Add honey or agave syrup and lime juice to the blender.
Blend the mixture until smooth and slushy.
Taste the slush and adjust the sweetness and acidity by adding more honey/agave or lime juice if needed.
If a thicker consistency is desired, add ice cubes and blend again until smooth.
Pour the Mango Moscato Slush into glasses.
Garnish with fresh mango slices.
Serve immediately and enjoy your Mango Moscato Slush!

Feel free to customize the recipe by using different varieties of Moscato or adding a splash of mango-flavored liqueur for extra mango richness. This frozen treat is perfect for warm days, tropical-themed parties, or any occasion where you want to enjoy the tropical flavors of mango and the sweetness of Moscato. Cheers!

Blueberry Lemon Wine Slush

Ingredients:

- 2 cups frozen blueberries
- 1 bottle (750 ml) white wine (such as Sauvignon Blanc or Pinot Grigio), chilled
- 2 tablespoons honey or agave syrup (adjust to taste)
- Juice of 2 lemons
- Ice cubes (optional)
- Fresh blueberries and lemon slices for garnish

Instructions:

Place the frozen blueberries in a blender.
Pour the chilled white wine into the blender with the blueberries.
Add honey or agave syrup and the juice of two lemons to the blender.
Blend the mixture until smooth and slushy.
Taste the slush and adjust the sweetness and acidity by adding more honey/agave or lemon juice if needed.
If a thicker consistency is desired, add ice cubes and blend again until smooth.
Pour the Blueberry Lemon Wine Slush into glasses.
Garnish with fresh blueberries and lemon slices.
Serve immediately and enjoy your Blueberry Lemon Wine Slush!

Feel free to customize the recipe by using different white wine varieties or adding a splash of blueberry-flavored liqueur for extra blueberry goodness. This frozen treat is perfect for summer gatherings or any occasion where you want to enjoy a burst of blueberry and lemon flavors. Cheers!

Raspberry Rosé Slushie

Ingredients:

- 2 cups frozen raspberries
- 1 bottle (750 ml) rosé wine, chilled
- 2 tablespoons sugar or honey (adjust to taste)
- 1-2 tablespoons lime juice
- Ice cubes (optional)
- Fresh raspberries and lime slices for garnish

Instructions:

Place the frozen raspberries in a blender.
Pour the chilled rosé wine into the blender with the raspberries.
Add sugar or honey and lime juice to the blender.
Blend the mixture until smooth and slushy.
Taste the slush and adjust the sweetness and acidity by adding more sugar/honey or lime juice if needed.
If a thicker consistency is desired, add ice cubes and blend again until smooth.
Pour the Raspberry Rosé Slushie into glasses.
Garnish with fresh raspberries and lime slices.
Serve immediately and enjoy your Raspberry Rosé Slushie!

Feel free to customize the recipe by using different varieties of rosé or adding a splash of raspberry liqueur for an extra burst of flavor. This frozen treat is perfect for warm days, summer parties, or any occasion where you want to savor the delicious combination of raspberries and rosé. Cheers!

Mango Strawberry Wine Slush

Ingredients:

- 1 cup frozen mango chunks
- 1 cup frozen strawberries
- 1 bottle (750 ml) white wine (such as Sauvignon Blanc or Pinot Grigio), chilled
- 2 tablespoons honey or agave syrup (adjust to taste)
- Juice of 1 lime
- Ice cubes (optional)
- Fresh mango slices and strawberries for garnish

Instructions:

Place the frozen mango chunks and frozen strawberries in a blender.
Pour the chilled white wine into the blender with the frozen fruits.
Add honey or agave syrup and the juice of one lime to the blender.
Blend the mixture until smooth and slushy.
Taste the slush and adjust the sweetness and acidity by adding more honey/agave or lime juice if needed.
If a thicker consistency is desired, add ice cubes and blend again until smooth.
Pour the Mango Strawberry Wine Slush into glasses.
Garnish with fresh mango slices and strawberries.
Serve immediately and enjoy your Mango Strawberry Wine Slush!

Feel free to customize the recipe by using different white wine varieties or adding a splash of mango or strawberry liqueur for an extra fruity kick. This frozen treat is perfect for summer gatherings or any occasion where you want to enjoy the tropical combination of mango and strawberries with a hint of wine. Cheers!

Unique Wine Beverages:

Mulled Wine

Ingredients:

- 1 bottle (750 ml) red wine (such as Cabernet Sauvignon or Merlot)
- 1/4 cup brandy or cognac (optional)
- 1/4 cup honey or sugar (adjust to taste)
- 1 orange, sliced
- 1 lemon, sliced
- 2 cinnamon sticks
- 3-4 whole cloves
- 3-4 star anise
- 1-2 cardamom pods (optional)
- 1 vanilla bean, split (optional)
- Orange zest for garnish

Instructions:

In a large saucepan, combine the red wine, brandy (if using), honey or sugar, orange slices, lemon slices, cinnamon sticks, cloves, star anise, cardamom pods (if using), and vanilla bean (if using).
Heat the mixture over medium heat until it reaches a simmer. Do not boil.
Reduce the heat to low and let the mulled wine simmer for 15-20 minutes to allow the flavors to meld.
Taste the mulled wine and adjust the sweetness by adding more honey or sugar if needed.
Strain the mulled wine to remove the spices and fruit slices.
Serve the mulled wine warm in mugs or heat-resistant glasses.
Garnish with orange zest and additional cinnamon sticks if desired.

Enjoy your comforting and spiced Classic Mulled Wine!

Feel free to customize the recipe by adding other spices like nutmeg or ginger, and you can also experiment with different types of red wine to suit your taste. Mulled wine is a festive and cozy drink that is perfect for holiday gatherings or chilly evenings. Cheers!

Wine Ice Pops

Ingredients:

- 1 bottle (750 ml) of your favorite wine (red, white, or rosé)
- 1/4 cup simple syrup (adjust to taste)
- Fresh fruit slices or berries (optional)
- Popsicle molds
- Popsicle sticks

Instructions:

In a mixing bowl, combine the wine and simple syrup. Stir well until the simple syrup is fully incorporated.
Taste the mixture and adjust the sweetness by adding more simple syrup if needed. Keep in mind that freezing dulls flavors, so the mixture should be a bit sweeter than you want the final popsicles to be.
If desired, add fresh fruit slices or berries to the mixture for added flavor and texture.
Pour the wine mixture into popsicle molds, leaving a little space at the top for expansion.
Insert popsicle sticks into the molds.
Place the molds in the freezer and let them freeze for at least 4-6 hours, or until completely solid.
Once frozen, remove the wine popsicles from the molds.
Serve and enjoy your Wine Ice Pops!

Tips:

- To easily remove the popsicles from the molds, briefly run the molds under warm water.
- Feel free to experiment with different wine varieties and fruit combinations.

These wine popsicles are a delightful and adult-friendly treat for summer gatherings, pool parties, or just a relaxing day in the sun. Cheers!

Wine Smoothie

Ingredients:

- 1 bottle (750 ml) of your preferred wine (rosé, white, or red)
- 2 cups frozen fruits (such as berries, peaches, or mixed fruits)
- 1-2 tablespoons honey or simple syrup (optional, adjust to taste)
- Ice cubes (optional, depending on your desired thickness)
- Fresh mint or citrus slices for garnish (optional)

Instructions:

Pour the wine into ice cube trays and freeze until solid. This step is optional but adds a slushier texture to the smoothie.
In a blender, combine the frozen wine cubes, frozen fruits, and honey or simple syrup.
Blend the mixture until smooth and slushy. If the consistency is too thick, you can add a few ice cubes and blend again.
Taste the smoothie and adjust the sweetness by adding more honey or simple syrup if needed.
Pour the Wine Smoothie into glasses.
Garnish with fresh mint or citrus slices if desired.
Serve immediately and enjoy your Wine Smoothie!

Feel free to get creative and customize your wine smoothie by experimenting with different wine varieties and fruit combinations. You can also add a splash of fruit juice or a flavored liqueur for an extra layer of flavor.

Wine smoothies are perfect for warm days, brunches, or any occasion where you want to enjoy a cool and fruity beverage with a hint of wine. Cheers!

Savory Wine Spritz

Ingredients:

- 1 bottle (750 ml) white wine (such as Sauvignon Blanc or Pinot Grigio), chilled
- 1 cup sparkling water or club soda, chilled
- 1/4 cup dry vermouth
- 1 tablespoon honey or agave syrup (adjust to taste)
- 1 lemon, thinly sliced
- Fresh herbs (such as thyme or rosemary)
- Ice cubes
- Optional: Cucumber slices for garnish

Instructions:

In a pitcher, combine the chilled white wine, sparkling water or club soda, and dry vermouth.

Add honey or agave syrup to the pitcher and stir until well combined. Adjust sweetness to taste.

Squeeze the juice from a few lemon slices into the mixture and drop the slices into the pitcher.

Add fresh herbs to the pitcher. If using thyme or rosemary, lightly muddle them to release their flavors.

Place the pitcher in the refrigerator and let it chill for at least 1-2 hours to allow the flavors to meld.

Just before serving, add ice cubes to the pitcher for a refreshing chill.

Pour the Savory Wine Spritz into glasses.

Garnish with additional lemon slices and optional cucumber slices.

Stir gently and serve your Savory Wine Spritz.

Feel free to experiment with different herbs and adjust the sweetness and acidity levels according to your preference. The combination of white wine, herbs, and a touch of sweetness creates a sophisticated and savory twist on the traditional wine spritzer. Enjoy!

Wine Hot Chocolate

Ingredients:

- 2 cups milk (whole or your preferred type)
- 1/2 cup red wine (such as Merlot or Cabernet Sauvignon)
- 1/4 cup unsweetened cocoa powder
- 1/4 cup granulated sugar (adjust to taste)
- 1/4 teaspoon vanilla extract
- A pinch of salt
- Whipped cream and chocolate shavings for garnish (optional)

Instructions:

In a saucepan over medium heat, combine the milk, red wine, cocoa powder, sugar, vanilla extract, and a pinch of salt.
Whisk the mixture continuously until it's well combined and heated through. Be careful not to let it boil.
Taste the hot chocolate and adjust the sweetness by adding more sugar if needed.
Once the hot chocolate is well combined and warmed to your liking, remove it from the heat.
Pour the red wine hot chocolate into mugs.
If desired, top each mug with whipped cream and chocolate shavings.
Serve immediately and enjoy your Red Wine Hot Chocolate!

Feel free to get creative with this recipe. You can experiment with different types of red wine or even add a splash of flavored liqueur like raspberry or orange for an extra layer of flavor. This indulgent beverage is perfect for cold evenings or as a luxurious treat during the holiday season. Cheers!

Wine Slush Float

Ingredients:

- 1 bottle (750 ml) of your favorite wine (red, white, or rosé)
- 2 cups frozen fruit (such as berries, peaches, or mixed fruits)
- 1/4 cup simple syrup (adjust to taste)
- 1-2 cups soda (club soda, ginger ale, or a flavored soda of your choice)
- Fresh fruit for garnish
- Ice cubes (optional)

Instructions:

Pour the wine into ice cube trays and freeze until solid. This step is optional but adds a slushier texture to the drink.
In a blender, combine the frozen wine cubes, frozen fruit, and simple syrup.
Blend the mixture until smooth and slushy. If the consistency is too thick, you can add a few ice cubes and blend again.
Taste the wine slush and adjust the sweetness by adding more simple syrup if needed.
Pour the wine slush into glasses, filling them about halfway.
Top each glass with soda, allowing it to create a fizzy and frothy layer on top of the slush.
Garnish with fresh fruit.
Serve immediately and enjoy your Wine Slush Float!

Feel free to experiment with different wine varieties, frozen fruits, and soda flavors to create your own unique combinations. This fun and festive drink is perfect for outdoor gatherings, brunches, or any occasion where you want to enjoy a wine slush with a fizzy twist. Cheers!

Spicy Jalapeño Wine Margarita

Ingredients:

- 1 1/2 oz silver tequila
- 1 oz triple sec or orange liqueur
- 1 oz fresh lime juice
- 1 oz simple syrup (adjust to taste)
- 1/2 oz jalapeño-infused red wine (see instructions below)
- Jalapeño slices for garnish
- Salt for rimming the glass (optional)
- Ice cubes

Jalapeño-Infused Red Wine:

- 1 cup red wine (such as Cabernet Sauvignon)
- 1-2 jalapeños, sliced (adjust to desired spiciness)

Instructions:

Jalapeño-Infused Red Wine:

In a small saucepan, heat the red wine over low-medium heat until it starts to simmer.
Add the sliced jalapeños and let them steep in the wine for about 15-20 minutes.
Remove from heat and let the mixture cool. Strain out the jalapeño slices, and the infused wine is ready.

Spicy Jalapeño Wine Margarita:

Rim the glass with salt (optional) by moistening the rim with a lime wedge and dipping it into salt.
In a shaker, combine tequila, triple sec, fresh lime juice, simple syrup, and jalapeño-infused red wine.
Add ice to the shaker and shake well to chill the ingredients.
Strain the mixture into the prepared glass filled with ice.
Garnish with jalapeño slices.
Serve immediately and enjoy your Spicy Jalapeño Wine Margarita!

Feel free to adjust the level of spice by adding more or fewer jalapeños to the infused wine. This cocktail offers a perfect balance of heat, sweetness, and citrusy brightness, making it a unique and flavorful choice for your next gathering. Cheers!

Lemon Lavender Wine Spritz
Ingredients:

- 1 bottle (750 ml) white wine (such as Sauvignon Blanc or Pinot Grigio), chilled
- 1/4 cup lavender simple syrup (recipe below)
- Juice of 2 lemons
- Sparkling water or club soda, chilled
- Ice cubes
- Fresh lavender sprigs and lemon slices for garnish

Lavender Simple Syrup:

- 1 cup water
- 1 cup granulated sugar
- 2 tablespoons dried culinary lavender

Instructions:

Lavender Simple Syrup:

In a saucepan, combine water, sugar, and dried lavender.
Bring the mixture to a simmer over medium heat, stirring until the sugar dissolves.
Let the syrup simmer for about 5 minutes to infuse the lavender flavor.
Remove from heat and let the syrup cool.
Strain out the dried lavender, and your lavender simple syrup is ready to use.

Lemon Lavender Wine Spritz:

In a pitcher, combine the chilled white wine, lavender simple syrup, and lemon juice. Stir well.
Fill glasses with ice cubes.
Pour the wine mixture over the ice in each glass, leaving some space at the top.
Top each glass with sparkling water or club soda to your liking.
Garnish with fresh lavender sprigs and lemon slices.
Stir gently and serve your Lemon Lavender Wine Spritz.

Feel free to adjust the sweetness by adding more or less lavender simple syrup, depending on your taste preferences. This spritz is perfect for outdoor gatherings, picnics, or any occasion where you want to enjoy a light and aromatic wine beverage. Cheers!

Wine Infused Lemonade

Ingredients:

- 1 bottle (750 ml) white wine (such as Sauvignon Blanc or Pinot Grigio), chilled
- 1 cup freshly squeezed lemon juice (about 4-6 lemons)
- 1/2 cup simple syrup (adjust to taste)
- 1 lemon, thinly sliced
- Ice cubes
- Fresh mint leaves for garnish (optional)

Instructions:

In a pitcher, combine the chilled white wine, freshly squeezed lemon juice, and simple syrup. Stir well to mix.
Add the thinly sliced lemon to the pitcher.
Place the pitcher in the refrigerator and let the mixture chill for at least 1-2 hours to allow the flavors to meld.
Fill glasses with ice cubes.
Pour the wine-infused lemonade over the ice in each glass.
Garnish with fresh mint leaves if desired.
Stir gently and serve your Wine-Infused Lemonade.

Feel free to customize the sweetness by adjusting the amount of simple syrup according to your taste preferences. You can also experiment with different white wine varieties to find your favorite combination.

This wine-infused lemonade is perfect for sunny days, picnics, or as a refreshing option for outdoor gatherings. It's a delightful balance of citrusy and wine flavors. Cheers!

Balsamic Berry Wine Reduction

Ingredients:

- 1 cup mixed berries (such as strawberries, blueberries, raspberries, or blackberries)
- 1/2 cup red wine (such as Merlot or Cabernet Sauvignon)
- 1/4 cup balsamic vinegar
- 2-3 tablespoons honey or maple syrup (adjust to taste)
- 1 teaspoon cornstarch (optional, for thickening)

Instructions:

In a small saucepan, combine the mixed berries, red wine, balsamic vinegar, and honey or maple syrup.
Bring the mixture to a simmer over medium heat, stirring occasionally.
Reduce the heat to low and let the berries simmer for about 10-15 minutes, or until the berries have softened and released their juices.
If you prefer a thicker consistency, mix the cornstarch with a tablespoon of water to create a slurry. Stir the slurry into the berry mixture and simmer for an additional 2-3 minutes until the sauce thickens.
Remove the saucepan from heat and let the balsamic berry reduction cool.
Once cooled, you can strain the sauce to remove the seeds if desired, or leave it as is for a chunkier texture.
Transfer the balsamic berry reduction to a jar or container for storage.
Use the reduction as a topping for desserts, salads, grilled meats, or any dish that could benefit from a burst of fruity and balsamic flavor.

This versatile reduction adds a delightful sweetness and acidity to a variety of dishes. It can be stored in the refrigerator for a week or more, making it a handy condiment for enhancing both sweet and savory dishes. Enjoy!

Wine-soaked Berries with Mascarpone

Ingredients:

- 2 cups mixed berries (strawberries, blueberries, raspberries, blackberries)
- 1/2 cup red wine (such as Merlot or Cabernet Sauvignon)
- 2-3 tablespoons honey or maple syrup (adjust to taste)
- 8 ounces mascarpone cheese, softened
- 1-2 tablespoons powdered sugar (adjust to taste)
- 1 teaspoon vanilla extract
- Fresh mint leaves for garnish (optional)

Instructions:

In a bowl, combine the mixed berries, red wine, and honey or maple syrup. Stir gently to coat the berries in the wine mixture.

Let the berries soak in the wine for at least 30 minutes to allow the flavors to meld. You can refrigerate them if desired.

In a separate bowl, whisk together the softened mascarpone cheese, powdered sugar, and vanilla extract until smooth and well combined.

Spoon the wine-soaked berries into serving glasses or bowls.

Dollop the mascarpone mixture over the berries.

Garnish with fresh mint leaves if desired.

Serve immediately and enjoy your Wine-Soaked Berries with Mascarpone.

This dessert is perfect for special occasions or as a delightful treat after a meal. The combination of wine-soaked berries and mascarpone creates a luscious and indulgent flavor experience. Feel free to customize the sweetness by adjusting the amount of honey or maple syrup according to your taste preferences. Cheers!

Hibiscus Rosé Punch

Ingredients:

- 1 bottle (750 ml) rosé wine, chilled
- 1 cup hibiscus tea, brewed and cooled
- 1/4 cup elderflower liqueur (optional)
- 1/4 cup simple syrup (adjust to taste)
- 1 cup sparkling water or club soda, chilled
- 1 orange, thinly sliced
- 1 lemon, thinly sliced
- Fresh berries (such as strawberries or raspberries) for garnish
- Ice cubes
- Fresh mint leaves for garnish (optional)

Instructions:

Brew hibiscus tea by steeping hibiscus tea bags in hot water according to package instructions. Let it cool completely.
In a large punch bowl or pitcher, combine the chilled rosé wine, hibiscus tea, elderflower liqueur (if using), and simple syrup. Stir well to mix.
Add the thinly sliced orange and lemon to the punch.
Just before serving, pour in the chilled sparkling water or club soda to add a fizzy touch. Adjust the sweetness with more simple syrup if needed.
Add ice cubes to the punch to keep it cool.
Garnish with fresh berries and, if desired, fresh mint leaves.
Stir gently to combine all the flavors.
Serve the Hibiscus Rosé Punch in glasses over ice.

This punch is not only visually stunning but also bursting with floral and fruity notes. It's perfect for spring and summer gatherings, brunches, or any occasion where you want to impress your guests with a refreshing and elegant drink. Cheers!

Pomegranate Wine Spritzer

Ingredients:

- 1 cup pomegranate juice, chilled
- 1 bottle (750 ml) red wine (such as Cabernet Sauvignon or Merlot), chilled
- 1 cup club soda or sparkling water, chilled
- 1-2 tablespoons simple syrup (adjust to taste)
- Fresh pomegranate arils for garnish
- Ice cubes
- Mint leaves for garnish (optional)

Instructions:

In a pitcher, combine the chilled pomegranate juice and red wine.
Add simple syrup to the mixture and stir well. Adjust the sweetness to your liking.
Just before serving, pour in the chilled club soda or sparkling water.
Fill glasses with ice cubes.
Pour the Pomegranate Wine Spritzer into each glass.
Garnish with fresh pomegranate arils and, if desired, mint leaves.
Stir gently to combine the flavors.
Serve immediately and enjoy your Pomegranate Wine Spritzer!

Feel free to customize the recipe by using white wine for a different flavor profile or adding a splash of citrus juice for extra freshness. This spritzer is perfect for holiday celebrations, parties, or any occasion where you want to enjoy a light and fruity wine drink. Cheers!

Chocolate Red Wine Truffles

Ingredients:

- 8 ounces (about 225 grams) dark chocolate, finely chopped
- 1/2 cup heavy cream
- 1/4 cup red wine (choose a red wine with rich and fruity notes)
- 2 tablespoons unsalted butter, softened
- Cocoa powder, powdered sugar, or finely chopped nuts for coating

Instructions:

Place the finely chopped dark chocolate in a heatproof bowl.

In a small saucepan, heat the heavy cream over medium heat until it just begins to simmer. Do not let it boil.

Pour the hot cream over the chopped chocolate and let it sit for a minute to melt the chocolate.

Gently stir the chocolate and cream until smooth and well combined.

Stir in the red wine and softened butter until the mixture is smooth and glossy.

Cover the bowl with plastic wrap and refrigerate the mixture for at least 3 hours or until firm.

Once the truffle mixture is firm, use a spoon or a melon baller to scoop out portions and roll them into small balls.

Roll each truffle in cocoa powder, powdered sugar, or finely chopped nuts to coat.

Place the coated truffles on a parchment-lined tray and refrigerate for another 30 minutes to set.

Store the chocolate red wine truffles in an airtight container in the refrigerator until ready to serve.

These truffles are a perfect indulgence for special occasions or as a homemade gift for chocolate and wine lovers. The combination of dark chocolate and red wine creates a luxurious and sophisticated flavor. Enjoy!

www.ingramcontent.com/pod-product-compliance
Lightning Source LLC
LaVergne TN
LVHW081509060526
838201LV00056BA/3024